Penny Ante Feud 15

Walking the Dog Star

Shoe
Music
Press

Penny Ante Feud 15: Walking the Dog Star is published by Shoe Music Press, Alpharetta, GA USA. Its contents are protected by copyright law where applicable.

Cover image: *Walking the Dog Star* by Ed Markowski

Penny Ante Feud has appeared in serial under ISSN: 2153-6422.

Email us at shoemusicpress@gmail.com and visit us online at www.shoemusicpress.com

Holly Day

Haunting

I close my eyes and pretend
that you're not in my
head, that when I close my
eyes I don't still see you. I close
my ears and pretend that
I don't recognize your
voice, that I don't remember
how
your breath

sounds when you sleep, that I don't remember
you. somehow you
got inside me and
I can't shake you
loose. somehow I have to find
some way to purify

myself of all the things
you put inside of
me. our last conversation
still floats through my dreams,
the cold creep of certainty
I felt when I knew it would be

our last, our last moments
as a couple. I could

(Continued on page 2)

see you pulling away
from me, even then, as
if in a dream, a
horrible dream, long
before you told me
you were leaving,

felt it as certain
as a door closing
between us.

Simon Perchik

Even these laces, breathless
falling to the floor without you
and the wait for calm—they cope

by helping you undress
used to shoes that weigh too much
are lowered forever, caressed

and still you talk non-stop
dangle your bare feet
half overboard, half

the way these enormous clothes
lose hold, break apart, then nothing
to heap one on top the other.

Joe DeMarco

Vagina Envy

The (not-so-little) mermaid stares down
between her scales,
to the spot where the sun don't shine.
A look of concern dawning on her face,
she can't help but wonder
(not what it might be like to have legs
or to walk and run)
but what it might be like to have a pussy
or Who-ha if pussy is too dirty.
She has vagina envy.
For although she has been
blessed with a bodacious pair of puppies,
or tatas or breasts if puppies and tatas offend you,
she feels incomplete with out the Who-ha
or cunt if Who-ha is too clean.
She saw the word in a dirty magazine,
that her friend gave her,
and now whenever she gets the chance,
she swims to the surface,
and stares at the pictures
of women spreading their meat curtains,
or showing off their honey pot, if meat curtains is too pejorative.
She fantasizes about having that bearded clam between her legs,
about taking her fingers and parting those luscious lips
perhaps fishing around down there
although she doesn't know why men use that term;
the vagina is not like a fish
it is more like a flower.

She stays in that spot,
studying and staring at where all life begins
envious that she herself
does not have a heart-shaped box.

Kristen A. Skerry

Rising from the Ashes

Not a soul can burn my wings.
Many have tried, including myself.
I am the heat of your Earth's core
come home to warm your hands.
For I am Forever. Eternal.
I am the Phoenix.
Blazing, not merely fading
to die out like the rest of us shall.
You will always sense me rising.
Soaring. Burning.
Closer to you now then you are to yourself.
A soul within a soul.
Rising. Everlasting.
An angel of the ashes
from the simmering embers
of summer evening campfire frivolity.
I am fluent in the speech of the Flame
and yet, for you, I am visceral.
Fear not to ever face life alone.
For you are silently shielded.
You have my Phoenix word.

<u>David Booth</u>

Today

Today isn't the day.
Trust me.
I've made many plans.
Please don't stop me.
Think of the people around us.
Yes, you can have my head today.
But if you wait until tomorrow,
you can have it then and also keep your own head about you.
Take your hands out of your pockets.
Walk away.
Walk away.

Ivan de Monbrison

A Surrealistic Dog

Weaning of the dumb wolves.
The hinge that ties each muscle to the bone makes it
easy for the arm to stretch out and to grasp
something invisible but so close at the same time.
We walk back to the edge of the void. Vertigo takes us
by the shoulder and tells us to get back within
ourselves.
At the first step you saw a man falling from the top of a cliff.
At the second step you saw this man yelling.
At the third step you saw this man coming out of his home
happy to go and get married, then harnessed to
two dead donkeys he was pulling a piano behind him
as well as two priests, one of them being a painter in
his spare time.
A wound opened in his hand and ants came out of it. In
the end we had to leave and eventually doze it off
among liquid watches. Between the rocks a dead man
spoke softly. You draw close to him. Backlighted the
vampires had filled the naves of these high cathedrals
with the shadows of their tall figures.
At the fourth step you came back to yourself. Out of
your dream you wanted to remember your name, but it
was impossible, litigious but so convenient amnesia.
At the fifth step you turned into this cat that is now
watching you from afar, this cat knows you so well that
if it could it would not hesitate to come and eat you up.

(Continued on page 10)

8

Sevrage des loups muets.

La charnière de chaque muscle avec l'os rend aisé le mouvement que fait le bras qui se tend comme pour saisir quelque chose d'invisible mais de si proche en même temps.

On recule au bord du vide. Le vertige nous prend par l'épaule et nous dit de nous retourner vers nous même.

Au premier pas tu as vu un homme tomber du haut d'une falaise. Au deuxième pas tu as vu cet homme hurler.

Au troisième pas tu as vu cet homme sortir de chez lui heureux d'aller se marier, ensuite harnaché à deux ânes morts il tirait un piano derrière lui ainsi que deux prêtres dont l'un était peintre à ses heures perdues.

Une plaie s'ouvrit dans sa main et des fourmis en sortirent. Il fallut aller finir par s'assoupir parmi l es montres liquides. Au milieu des rochers un mort parlait tout bas. Tu t'en es approché. Les ombres des vampires avaient rempli les nefs de ces hautes cathédrales à l'aide du contre-jour de leurs silhouettes immenses.

Au quatrième pas tu es revenu jusqu'à toi même. Tu es sorti de ton rêve et tu as voulu te souvenir de ton nom mais c'était impossible, amnésie litigieuse mais si pratique.

Au cinquième pas tu es devenu ce chat qui t'observe de loin, qui te connaît si bien mais qui, s'il le pouvait, n'hésiterait pas à venir te dévorer.

(Continued on page 11)

Now leave me alone... The alliance of the king and the
queen can not wait any longer.
The key has enabled us to move in the palace by the
passage of desire, to push the door and find the
staggering landscape of love.
The stranger greets us with his palms open as sour
apples and his eyes offered to the stars.
Horses were having fun in a field which was
green as green can be, like a new season,
like oblivion,
like beauty.
Children were climbing on trees.
At the first moment of your birth,
Being just out of yourself.
Nude lips.
You have offered the world to your intelligence and
everything went away.

A présent laissez moi... L'alliance de la reine et du
roi ne saurait souffrir de retard.
La clé nous a permis d'entrer dans ce palais par le
passage du désir, d'en pousser la porte et de découvrir le
sidérant paysage de l'amour.
L'étranger nous accueille avec ses paumes ouvertes comme de pommes
sures et ses yeux offerts aux étoiles.
Des chevaux s'amusaient dans un champs aussi
vert qu'il se peut, vert comme une saison nouvelle,
comme l'oubli,
comme la beauté.
Des enfants grimpaient dans les arbres.
Au premier instant de ta naissance,
A peine issu de toi-même.
Les lèvres nues.
Tu as offert le monde à ton intelligence
et tout a disparu.

Bray McDonald

Poetic Catharsis
(In Memory of J. Daniel Byford)

Over the years and across the miles
that have taken up my life and time
I must have missed something important,
or caught something like a virus.
So I'm forgetting everything I ever learned
so I may wonder in the awe of now;
and forsaking my knowledge of me
and the world spins slowly on an invisible thread.

I must have misplaced something rare,
or gave something away that I should have kept
on this voyage through time's tunnel of despair
that has left my life a pock-marked reflection.
So I'm burying everything I ever uncovered
beneath a bleak and barren brae
as the restless stars stir in their suspension
and the world spins slowly on an invisible thread.

The mirror reflects something I don't understand;
something familiar but truly unknown.
Trying to find an elusive cause or cure for what ails it.
So I'm disbelieving everything I believed
for the truth that faith steals and the drama of clarity
as the night drips down towards dawn
and the wind rises with the setting moon
and the world spins slowly on an invisible thread.

Michael M. Marks

Dogs Turned into Cats

Dye in the sky whiter than white,
wetter than white and hardly a hurt to me.
I did my cleverbest monkeytest
to tell the hell from the handbags.
I fought my thoughts of convention,
and bought a box of retention locks.
Dogs turned into cats,
but were banana peels on the way.
Hello nouveau, goodbye red-eye;
I don't yet know You nova Jehovah,
although You're mostly the show
too slow to explode the code
of awe I saw in Arkansas
on a missing Sunday morning.

Afrose Fatima Ahmed

Missed Opportunities

Every instant is an invitation
from the universe
to take part in eternity
and we are constantly saying,
    No, thanks.

B. Joseph Biesek

As For Me and As For Spain

I see the sky, watch the relic days.
Seeing which bathtub contains nothing.
A cusp of nothing is everything. I blame
Hart Crane, and myself, I am happy
for Spain. We are warring, every
day, Spain, and, America. Weren't,
once, we friends? Fellow animals?
I am happy, for
Spain. Wild-eyed mothers buying plasticine,
distracted, inky drinks. This is pure-
violence, soiled by-and-within one
system. A lie is being built-up, of
concept. I give up, the lies adjust,
build-up. A flow, in, this,
mezzanine. Will she be mine?
Will she ever be mine? This is
so ridiculous, I say; my friend,
though, encourages me. Music
blares, hear me out, who sent them
around midnight? America
in Spain, of course.

Craig Kurtz

A System of Seasons

If I could
I would chose
all the seasons
next to you.

First comes spring
with dew-drop feet,
expanding clouds
suggest accomplishment;
the coffee's on,
the air is new,
your stride is strong:
the odds gets launched.

Now summer comes
from colors primed,
a world to etch
and animate;
a lunch of health
aims stints apace,
your crest is coined
from orb transformed.

Then fall arrives
with wide enclaves
of plans to frame
in expert light;
your hands ply thoughts

from fertile sight
to edit earth
as muscles flexed.

Soon, too soon,
the frost decrees
an apex reached
at dinner's chord;
your meed resolves
entelechy, this planet
bears your signature:
now rest replete.

If I could
I would chose
all these systems
right with you.

Peter Victor

Crosscurrents

"Long time since I've seen you Mon"

Petey had been watching me approach
It was a long walk
A monstrous block of concrete
Stretching out into the white and turquoise ocean
Under the hot Central American sun

The dock

Petey was a driver
A mountain village
Ramshackle cars
Dirt roads
And lots of drugs

A dangerous place

Petey was somewhere around sixty
He had one and a half arms
A worn face
And an easy smile
I never asked

"Do you want to go to Maria's?
She knows you are here"

We sat at the bar
Cold beer
A dirt floor
A black open sky
A long thick black braid

On my mind

They came in sometime after midnight
Three
Dead sober
And sat at the bar

Maria shifted
Watching my eyes
Petey appeared out of nowhere
Standing next to me in silence

Long minutes went by as I watched the contorting faces
Feeling the stress rise
"Petey, I need you right outside the door"
He walked out
Maria at his side

Long minutes went by
The exit was fast

Spinning tires
The air filled with dust and gravel
A long fast ride

(Continued on page 20)

19

As I watched the following headlights
From the back seat

Running through the check point
My papers held high
Kids with assault rifles
Wide eyed
As I ran under the big sign
PTP
Petroleum Terminal of Panama

Days later
Pacing the bridge
Speaking in low tones
We all listened to a crackling radio

As the space shuttle fell to earth

Ingrid Calderon

we got time

you got that curve
that slick
that way
of tracing down straight lines
and sucking out my sleep
techniques of barred
sweet tongues extracting devils
without warning

in morning rituals
of wine and weed
and in-between
my legs you speak

call and response
and muted apogees
your sweet face luring
deep in my marrow
contracting pleasure
sinister tales
of beatings ending
in sweet revenge

warm baths and laughs
shampoo and cigarettes
if this aint love
not sure what is

Daniel von der Embse

Solitary heart

In our wedding pictures,
the scar above my lip
recalls our difficult birth,
the sparring of wills
ultimately ending in a draw.
On our last day together,
I hold your fist in my hand
able no longer to be happy
in your company,
carrying this solitary heart
to where it can rest,
never again to feel so alone
as when we were together.

Johnny Payne

Bad Penny

What good to brake for a skunk?
Either way, the perfume will follow
You home. Already you spilled
Coffee on your shirt as the Dog Star
Ascends. Hot caffeine on a summer
Night makes no sense. You might
As well have gotten drunk since
You swerved anyway, as if you
Could avoid minor disaster.
Each morning, donut in hand
You make the sign of the cross
As you stoop to pick up a bad penny
Wondering who left it the night before.
So many signs to follow: a red bird
On a black wire, dry patch on a green
Lawn, the emoticon sent without a text.
On every shirt, a button lost, on
Every clearance rack an ashtray
From your past. You taught the cat
To spell but she can't remember the vowels.
In the dead of a nap, a small still voice
Tells you the oven has been left on
And grasshoppers invade your lawn.
An electrician's house call and a fortune
Teller's prophecy cost the same, seventy-five

(Continued on page 24)

Bucks. Choose now or later, for it will
Come to an equal end. The lucky dollar
You earned as your first restaurant
Tip will remain forever inside the left front
Pocket of pressed pants you left in a dry cleaners
Whose name you can't remember.

Chris Miller

Permanence

I believe in
Tompkins Sq Park in August 1991 and
bright Les Paul guitars under stage lights,
Lisa's brown round bottom by
the light in the hall, taking
six hours of French for eight weeks and her
wet feet on the institutional tile when she
walked nude back to her room from the
showers through the empty dormitory
passages, a white towel
wrapped around her head, just
trying to stay cool. I believe

in band practice and diners at 3 am. The
Yankees on the radio were so bad,
the late night AM losses on California road
trips. And kissing Lisa in her room,
the sheet under us, and the uniform
she wore waitressing on a wire hanger by
the door, next to the table fan, the ruffle on
the shoulder. The shape of
her breasts in my hard hands the taste of
Clove cigarettes and Southern Comfort
on our fingers.

(Continued on page 26)

Also the Delaware River and
the leather jacket I bought in
Philadelphia with the money I
saved from grinding stumps
all summer, what I would need
all winter, after the sets of teeth
chewed the discs down to
chips and splinters, down to the dirt
down to a Summer so polished I could
love it like church.

Ed Markowski

Stock Boy

One morning that January I was putting up the produce at Tringali's Market snow coming down thicker and heavier than a lead vest wind raging straight razor sharp when I opened a crate of sugar plums from Brazil I was looking at her lips she was standing barefoot smiling and sipping a coke barefoot in the blizzard she walked toward me she said southern and sultry boy you're about to get a kiss that'll make all them sugar plums taste more like vinegar than vinegar we closed our eyes when I opened mine there was nothing other than wave after wave after wave of wicked windsnow.

t. kilgore splake

darkness into light

early morning
first dawn shadows
turning tranny miles north
time for trekking
leaving quiet footsteps
climbing cliffs summit
crossing brautigan creek
recalling papa hem favorite
across the river
and into the trees
solitary poet
whiskey soaked brain
moving slowly
out of body consciousness
not like others
ant farm beehive drones
dawn to dusk
doing same old same
or tartt's goldfinch
cage chained ankle
always landing in same place
listening to forest ghosts
old copper miners
big lake seamen
lumberjacks and trappers
finnish farmers
tilling hard-scrabble soils
young native warriors

children lost
hot diphtheria fevers
better companions
than living cadavers
stupid petty voices
not missing woman
sacred profane passions
adriana of dreams
"renata" safe for papa
sad females
full of past resentments
collected from junior high
constant naggy complaints
numbing creative visions
leaving unpublished books
lost in literary shadows
moving up path
passing young pines
needles softly purring
old meadow with
thimbleberries in season
deep blue sky
thin clouds across horizon
hawks eagles falcons
soaring on warm thermals
reaching escarpment heights
standing at world's edge
thinking about beyond
wondering what's next
knowing i'll be here forever

(Continued on page 30)

dave engel scattering
funeral ashes and bones
afternoon light fading
racing night
back down cliffs
retrieving pickup truck
crockpot madness stew
bard res dinner waiting
before lost in darkness
like prisoner of tri-xxxy neg
keeping eyes open
for mountain lion
like matthiessen's snow leopard
another pure spirit

D.S. Maolalai

what I miss the most

is getting to sleep wrapped up together in that little bed you had
in that little house in Bayside
just around the corner from the Coast Road
and so near to Dollymount Strand
that you could almost taste what the sea smelled like,
and knowing that we would wake up together
at the same time
as the sun coming in
and that we would kiss our salted lips
and our hands
and I miss your long hair in my face all morning
and the toothiness of the smile on your pillow
and the knees raising the blankets beside me
and how I could still tell
whether or not
I was making you happy.

T.H. Cayne

Untitled Poem

The phone rang. Again.
He never felt so tired.
(Left. Pains. Chest.)

He knew he could never sleep again because of the dreams.
In which he disappeared in darkness. Every day.
(Pains. Heart. Explodes.)

Fear had taken him by so much surprise.
He was a hostage now.
(And it was getting so much closer.)

The constant ringing made him mad.
It had gotten louder by the years.

(And why would someone want to speak to him?
The sad excuse for a man, secluded, drown in alcohol and
its typical bitterness. Missing things. And not wanting to
think about the reason. Long ago.
And still.)

(Perhaps he needed to talk to someone?
Perhaps that would do good.
Nobody knows.)

He stared at the walls of the windowless room (he never felt so tired).

And picked up the receiver.

Michael Estabrook

Life Cycle

OK so I complained like crazy
about the miserable winter
we had here in New England
what with the constant snow
and ice storms, snow shovels,
ice scrappers, snowblowers,
ice melt, salt and sand, plows
and sand trucks, the cabin fever
raging within over the long dark
cold months turning us into
virtual wild and slavering beasts!

So now what, with spring
and summer looming in all their life-
giving glory: lawn mowers, fertilizers,
rakes, mouse traps, moles, mosquitoes
and gnats, poison ivy, wasp spray...
ah the great cycle of life goes on and on
and so does my complaining,
what can you do!

Laura Bernstein-Machlay

Some High School Boys I Remember

My contrary, my barefaced lies,
refusing to stay put, to wear
the same hands for three hours at a time.
I recognize you in the sideways between street signs, between
bank and vet and work, the drop off and retrieval
of my daughter from play date and kindergarten. I go on looking
in bad light, though my glasses are made of sand
and show choppy home movies in my peripheral vision.

Because you weigh a ton, because I remember your taste,
the warp and woof of you beneath the planes of my palms.
You, twelfth grade crush
who danced me punk rock crazy over the sunrise
and you, stoned boy leaning slow languid against
the institutional walls, stars-and-stripes boy
who couldn't get it up in my sandpaper insides. Boys
and boys. You understand,
I'm long married, sure in this truth that owes nothing
to clenched-belly, to glass shavings under my whole skin.
My name is on mortgage and credit card, my face
nearly my own.

And still I want to pull aside the car, lock-step
stumble across the pavement.
I want to pluck them from history,
take them in my arms, kiss and touch them everywhere
with tricks I've learned over this half-lifetime
until they moan low in their bodies, these boys
sidling into my passenger side, unbelted
of course, nudging my shoulder, my ribcage, to make me yelp,
jump a little in my seat.

Stubborn boys in your refusal to fade,
to quit laughing at me, at this wide stupid world.
Tell me a secret, then. One little horoscope come true.
Tell me a sin, just a small one,
to last the ride home.

New to Penny Ante Feud? You'll want to catch up on our back issues:

Please check our website www.shoemusicpress.com for current pricing (special bulk discount and author pricing available).